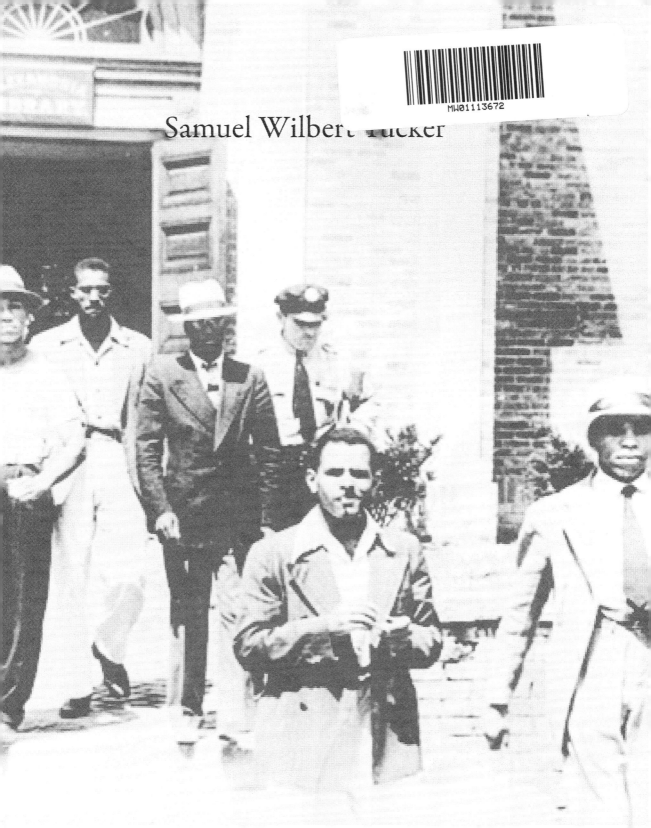

Samuel Wilbert Tucker

Samuel Wilbert Tucker

Samuel Wilbert Tucker

The Story of a Civil Rights Trailblazer
and the 1939 Alexandria Library Sit-In

Nancy Noyes Silcox

Reading brings opportunities!
Nancy Noyes Silcox

Published by Noysil Books
Arlington, Virginia

Samuel Wilbert Tucker:
The Story of a Civil Rights Trailblazer
and the 1939 Alexandria Library Sit-In

By Nancy Noyes Silcox

Published by Noysil Books
Arlington, Virginia
www.nancynoyessilcox.com

ISBN 978-1-934285-20-6
Library of Congress Control Number: 2013945810

Printed in the United States of America
First Edition, Fourth Printing

Maps: Robert E. Pratt
Cover Design: Jan Balderson
Index: History4All, Inc., Fairfax, Virginia
Manufacturing: Allegra, Dulles, Virginia

Dedicated
**to the students and teachers at
Samuel W. Tucker Elementary School
Alexandria, Virginia**

TABLE OF CONTENTS

FOREWORD

S.W. Tucker is a true unsung hero of the civil rights struggle in Virginia and in the nation.

This book provides a concise and accurate description of Tucker's life with emphasis on his legal contributions to the Civil Rights Movement.

I was privileged and honored to work closely with Tucker from May 5 of 1961 until his death in October of 1990.

My mother died when I was five years old, and I have very little memory of her. My father died in 1976. From then until October of 1990, Tucker and his wife Julia were like parents to me and my family. The Tuckers were a loving couple. They proved to be an excellent role model for us.

This is the first book I have seen about Tucker's life. I commend Nancy Noyes Silcox for doing an outstanding job.

Henry L. Marsh, III
Richmond, Virginia

CHAPTER 1

Early Life and Family

Samuel Wilbert Tucker was born in Alexandria, Virginia, on June 18, 1913. He had two brothers and a sister. His brother George was three years older. Brother Otto was three years younger. His sister Elsie, was almost six years younger.

His mother's name was Fannie L. Williams. She grew up on her father's farm in Fauquier County, west of Alexandria. Even as a young girl, she loved teaching. She practiced on her younger brothers and sisters. She graduated from Virginia Normal and Industrial Institute in Ettrick, a historically black college. Then she taught all grades in a one-room

901 Princess Street, the location of Samuel Wilbert Tucker's father's real estate office. Photographed in 2013

school for black children in Midland, Virginia. After getting married, she stayed home to take care of her growing family.

His father, Samuel A. Tucker, Jr., was born in Alexandria. During his life, he worked at many jobs. He was an insurance agent and a bartender. He ran a grocery store and a restaurant. For many years, he drove the car for George T. Klipstein, an Alexandria doctor. By 1924 he owned an office building near the family's house. Here he ran his own real estate business. His friend, Thomas M. Watson, practiced law in the same office.

Samuel A. Tucker, Jr.'s report card.

School was very important to the Tucker family. They believed reading meant freedom. Young Tucker learned to read before he started school. His father bought books and brought them home. His mother read to the children regularly. He, his brothers, and his sister benefited from his mother's training as a teacher.

His father had a huge desire to learn and saved his own third grade report card from the Snowden School for Boys because he was proud of his high marks. His father continued his

**Zion Baptist Church, 714 South Lee Street, Alexandria, Virginia.
Tucker's father grew up at 702 South Lee Street.**
Photographed in 2012

The autoharp was a popular instrument to accompany singing. Buttons were pressed to play chords when the strings were strummed.

education by going to law school at night. He wanted to become a lawyer. He took the bar exam several times, but didn't pass the test to get his license.

Young Tucker's father worked hard to improve his community. Because there was no decent public school for black children in Alexandria, he and other parents pressured the city to build Parker-Gray School in 1920. In 1939, he helped start Hopkins House, a community center with a child care program.

The family worshiped at Zion Baptist Church in Alexandria every Sunday. It was a church where everyone cared about all the children, not just their own. Young Tucker's father was superintendent of the Sunday School. He also was choir director.

The whole Tucker family loved music and loved to sing. Young Tucker played the piano and the autoharp. He was in many church plays and programs. Being on stage prepared him for arguing court cases in front of a judge and jury. He said he learned "to stand on my feet and say what needs to be said."

CHAPTER 2

Queen Street Neighborhood

When Samuel Tucker was growing up, Alexandria was a segregated city. Black people and white people lived in separate areas.

Their children attended separate schools. They worshiped at separate churches. White restaurants did not serve African Americans. Restrooms and water fountains were labeled "colored" and "white." People sat in separate places on buses and streetcars. They saw movies in separate theatres, or sat in separate parts of the same theatre. They swam at separate beaches and pools.

In Alexandria, African Americans lived in certain neighborhoods. Many lived in rented houses that were run down because landlords didn't want to fix them

Jim Crow

Homer Plessy, a free man who was 7/8 white and 1/8 black, was jailed and fined for refusing to leave a "whites only" train car. Judge John Howard Ferguson decided the original case against Plessy. In 1896, the U.S. Supreme Court decided in *Plessy v. Ferguson* that separate places for blacks and whites were legal as long as they were equal.

This "separate but equal" way of life was called Jim Crow, after a character in a minstrel (variety) show. Separate was not equal. African Americans did not have equal opportunities in housing, work, travel, or education. *Plessy v. Ferguson* legalized racial discrimination.

up. The Tucker family owned their own home. It was a two-story, tan brick house in the Uptown section, north of King Street. It was a large, comfortable home with a fireplace and a small backyard.

The Queen Street neighborhood was racially mixed. Black families lived on both sides of the Tucker house. Black families and white families lived in the next block and around the corner. The Duncans, a white family, owned the pharmacy on the corner of Queen and Patrick. They lived next to their pharmacy. It was an urban neighborhood with business, churches, and homes next to each other.

People considered Queen Street the main business street for blacks. King Street was for whites. People followed laws and rules that limited the mixing of the two races. Most white Southerners believed this was the way it should be. This Jim Crow way of life was supposed to be "separate but equal." For African Americans, separate places usually were not equal.

Northwest Pharmacy
924 Queen Street
Photographed in 2012

Tucker Home at 916 Queen Street

Alexandria, VA
Photographed in 2013

Royal Meat Market
300 North Patrick Street
Photographed in 2013

The "separate but equal" Jim Crow laws sometimes confused children. Black children and white children played together until it was time to go to school or church. Then they were expected to go their own separate ways. They played kickball, baseball, marbles, ring-around-the-rosy, and hide-and-seek. One day, when playing hide-and-seek, Tucker's sister Elsie

Capitol Theater was built here around 1934.
Photographed in 2012

wandered to King Street. Doug Duncan, who was white, spotted her and brought her safely home. Elsie remembered that neighbors cared about each other. The Duncans were like part of the family. "When my mother was very sick, Mrs. Duncan would come and bring food, or find out if there was anything she could do to help," Elsie said.

Samuel Tucker lived in the house on Queen Street until he was 33 years old. Long after he was grown up, he still called the Queen Street neighborhood "my little world."

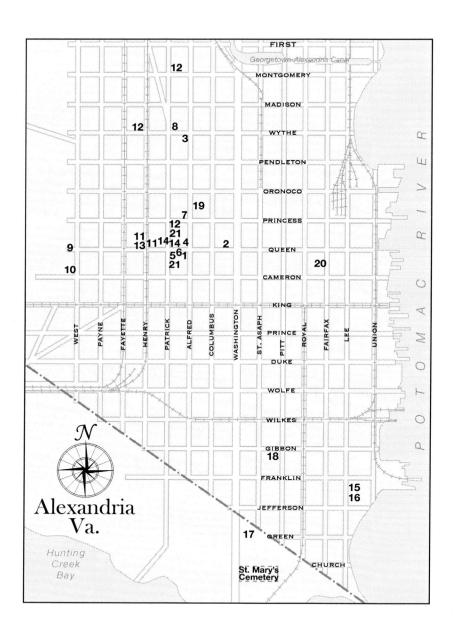

Henry and Oronoco streets, 1920

King and Pitt streets, 1926

Queen Street Neighborhood Map Key

1. Tucker house, 916 Queen Street.
2. Alexandria Library, 717 Queen Street.
3. Robert Robinson Library, 638 North Alfred Street.
4. Ebenezer Baptist Church, 909 Queen Street.
5. Northwest Pharmacy, 924 Queen Street.
6. Duncan house, 922 Queen Street.
7. Samuel A. Tucker, Jr.'s real estate office, Thomas Watson's law office, and S.W. Tucker's law office, 901 Princess Street.
8. Parker-Gray School, 901 Wythe Street.
9. Jefferson High School, 300 North West Street.
10. Alexandria High School, Cameron and North West streets.
11. Grocery stores (white-owned) 1007, 1023, and 1101 Queen Street.
12. Grocery stores (black-owned) 712 North Henry Street, and 313 and 901 North Patrick Street. Tucker's father and his friends ran the grocery at 313 North Patrick in 1920.
13. 1101 Queen Street. Site of a white-owned grocery store in 1915. By 1924, was the location of the Lincoln Theater. By 1934, replaced with the Capitol Theater.
14. Royal Meat Market (white-owned), 300 North Patrick Street, relocated to 301 North Patrick Street in 1941.
15. Tucker's father's family home, 702 South Lee Street.
16. Zion Baptist Church, 714 South Lee Street.
17. School where Tucker went for first grade. It was in the 900 block of South Washington Street across from St. Mary Catholic Church Cemetery.
18. Snowden School for Boys, 600 South Pitt Street.
19. Hallowell School for Girls, 413 North Alfred Street.
20. Alexandria Police and Corporation Courts, 126 and 132 North Fairfax Street.
21. Funeral homes (black-owned): John T. Rhines & Co. 221 North Patrick Street; W.C. Arnold, 311 North Patrick Street.

Parker-Gray School (circa 1920)
901 Wythe Street

Parker-Gray School had 675 students in grades 1-7 when it opened in 1920. Eighth grade was added in 1927. It was named for principals at the earlier Snowden School for Boys and Hollowell School for Girls, John F. Parker and Sarah J. Gray. The first principal was Henry T. White.

Parker-Gray cost $70,000 to build with tan brick inside and red brick outside. Twelve large classrooms had hooks for coats, large windows, and blackboards. However, there were 40 students in each classroom and 6 more classes than rooms. It was already overcrowded when it opened. There were classrooms for sewing and cooking taught by volunteer pupils from Armstrong High School in DC. The basement under each wing had bathrooms and a room for activities. An auditorium was on the ground floor.

Teachers had little schooling beyond high school, but an average of 20 years teaching experience. Students learned reading, spelling, grammar, and arithmetic.

CHAPTER 3

School Days

Samuel Tucker went to segregated schools in Alexandria, Virginia. When he was about four years old, he went to a private preschool near his house. Then he walked 14 blocks to attended first grade in a two-room school. He enjoyed that long walk down Washington Street. His first grade teacher was Laura Dorsey.

When Parker-Gray School opened in 1920, it was only four blocks from his house. He began second grade there. He skipped fifth grade after passing the fifth grade test, and went right into sixth grade. His sixth grade teacher was Rozier D. Lyles.

Parker-Gray School stopped at eighth grade. Black students had no high school in Alexandria. White students attended Alexandria's Jefferson High School. Jefferson was only four blocks from Tucker's house. For high school, he rode the streetcar into Washington, DC. Every school day, he rode the streetcar past his white friends' high school.

After the ride from Alexandria, he got off

Laura Dorsey

the streetcar in southwest Washington. Then he walked almost 2½ miles to Armstrong High School. The walk took about an hour, twice a day. Tucker knew it was wrong that he could not go to high school in Alexandria. Why did he think it was wrong? Because his father paid taxes just like every Alexandria citizen.

At Armstrong, he loved Mr. Ferguson's architectural and mechanical drawing class. He decided he wanted to be an architect. He had a habit of keeping a pencil balanced behind his ear. He was always prepared! Tucker graduated from high school in 1929. He was only 16 years old.

Then he went to Howard University. He joined the debate team and learned the power of fighting with words. Debating trained him to make logical, forceful, yet polite arguments. In July 1933, Tucker graduated from Howard with a bachelor's degree in Liberal Arts. He was only 20 years old.

When Tucker graduated from Howard, he was more interested in law than architecture. He loved putting words together to win a debate. He said listening to arguments in a courtroom was thrilling. He delighted in researching interesting topics. Also, he had been reading law books since he was ten years old. As he got older, Tucker helped his father's friend Tom Watson research and prepare cases in Watson's Alexandria law office.

Now he had a decision to make. Many students continued at Howard University's Law School, but Tucker decided he didn't want

> **Did you know?**
>
> In the 1830s, laws passed in Southern states made it illegal for anyone to teach slaves to read and write. Some people did, but they had to be careful. After the Civil War, Virginia established public schools to educate all children. These schools were segregated.

Howard University's Varsity Debate team.
Tucker is third from the right.

TUCKER, SAMUEL WILBERT
"Tommy Tucker"   Φ Β Σ
        916 Queen Street, Alexandria, Va.

Liberal Arts: A.B.
Armstrong High School, Washington, D. C.
Alpha Sigma Achievement Society; Chairman Com-
mittee on Religious Life, 4; Student Council Corresponding Secretary, 4; Kappa Sigma Debating Society; Secretary, 3; President, 4; Vice-President Political Science Club, 4; "Bison" Staff, 4; Sergeant Major
R. O. T. C., 3; Captain Co. A., 4; Corresponding
Secretary Inter-Collegiate Social Science Conference,
3; Class Debate, 2; Coach, 4; Varsity Debate, 3, 4;
Varsity Debate Key, 3.

His senior photograph in Howard University's yearbook,
***Bison* (1933)**

to go to law school "broke" (with no money). Instead, he studied for the bar exam—the test you need to pass to become a lawyer—on his own. Oliver Hill, his friend from Howard University, came over to study with Tucker on Thursdays.

They both took and passed the bar exam in December. Tucker was only 20½ years old. So he had to wait until he was 21 (legally an adult) to become a lawyer in Virginia. He was sworn into the Virginia State Bar on July 2, 1934, a few weeks after his 21st birthday.

Tucker's father in front of the office building, 901 Princess Street, where Young Tucker ran errands, typed, and studied law. The sign painted on the door was added after S.W. was sworn in as a lawyer on July 2, 1934.

Once he started practicing law with Tom Watson in Alexandria, he began calling himself S.W. Tucker. When Watson died unexpectedly in December, Lawyer Tucker took on Watson's clients, too. His first court trial was a murder case.

What's your name?

Samuel Wilbert Tucker used different names at different times and with different people. To his family he was Wilbert because his father's first name was also Samuel. His father's friend Tom Watson called him "Mr. Wilbert." At Howard University he had the nickname "Tommy Tucker," perhaps after the boy in the nursery rhyme who didn't have much money and "sang for his supper." When he became a lawyer, he called himself S.W. Tucker. To the people he represented in court, he was Attorney Tucker or Lawyer Tucker. His wife, Julia, called him Tucker; so did his law partner, Henry Marsh. Some friends simply called him Sam.

CHAPTER 4

Experiences Shape the Man

Besides his mother, Samuel Tucker talked about four men who greatly influenced his life.

SAMUEL A. TUCKER, JR.—HIS FATHER

Samuel A. Tucker loved learning and music. When his children were young, he traveled into Washington to study law at a night school. He bought books and brought them home for his children to read. At Zion Baptist Church, he held every position except being the pastor. His son Samuel remembered words from an old song his father always sang, "We've fought every race's battle,

When Young Tucker was in elementary school, his father continued his education at night school at Frelinghuysen University's John M. Langston School of Law in Washington, DC.

typewriter

but our own . . . fighting till we set our own race free." The song went on, "Always ready for battle when there's fighting work to do." Years later Tucker said, "These powerful words became part of me as a child."

G. DAVID WILLIAMS—HIS GRANDFATHER

Samuel Wilbert Tucker spent summers on the farm of his mother's father. The farm was near Midland, Virginia. Eggs and chickens from the farm were sold at the grocery store Tucker's father ran in Alexandria. One day, when his father and grandfather were talking, he overheard his grandfather say, "That was before they Jim Crowed us." From this, Tucker learned the Jim Crow segregation laws that separated the races "had not always been, were not God ordained, and did not always have to be."

THOMAS M. WATSON—HIS LAW MENTOR

When Samuel Tucker was about 10 years old, he ran errands and answered the telephone for his father and lawyer Tom Watson in the office they shared. He loved reading law books. He wanted to know how cases were decided. The office had a brand-new Royal typewriter that he was told not to touch, but he was curious. He read the instructions and learned how to type. He soon began doing more typing work than the office secretary did!

When Tucker was about 13 years old, Tom Watson trusted him to prepare documents he would use in court. Watson left details about cases. Tucker would get the correct papers ready. When he was in college, Watson would outline the facts of a case. Then Tucker would go to the Library of Congress to do the research. He said later that this was probably the main reason he became a lawyer. He also said he "grew up in that law office like a kid with two fathers, each one expecting me to take over their business."

ROZIER D. LYLES—HIS TEACHER

Rozier D. Lyles was Tucker's sixth grade teacher at Parker-Gray School. He said he was the best teacher he ever had. Lyles taught him everything he ever learned about the rules of English grammar. Good grammar skills helped him speak clearly in court and write correctly so everyone could understand his legal arguments. What he learned from Lyles as a young boy would help him win civil rights cases as a grown man.

Rozier D. Lyles

DISCRIMINATION

Discrimination was a regular reminder for African Americans that they were considered "second class citizens." One day when Young Samuel was about eight years old, he went to a white family his father knew to do some little job. At lunchtime, he was sent out to the porch to eat his lunch. The white children ate inside the house. When he told his mother, she said that he would not be going back there anymore.

When he was 14, he had his first experience with the legal system.

He was riding the streetcar back to Virginia from Washington, DC. He was with his brothers, George and Otto, and a friend. In segregated streetcars, blacks boarded from the back and sat in the back. Whites boarded from the front and sat in the front. The seats had moveable backs that could slide back and forth so a passenger could ride facing the front or the back of the streetcar.

Corporation Court in Alexandria, where the streetcar incident trial occurred.
Photographed in 2013

Samuel and George slid the back of a seat facing the white section to face the black section so Otto and their friend could ride facing them. A white woman, who had walked past empty seats in the white section, asked the boys to give up their seats. She wanted to turn the seat back around to face the white section. The boys refused. She gave up and sat in an empty seat in the white section.

CITY OF ALEXANDRIA

VS. { WARRANT

Geo Tucker and
Wm Tucker,

EXECUTED BY ARRESTING THE WITHIN NAMED

Geo Tucker fined $5 O-cts 3 costs
appeal noted June 27. Bond
in sum of $75 by O Cl
Tucker.

Wm Tucker fined 5 and
3 costs. appeal noted
personal Bond for appeal
J W Burroughs
Clerk Police Court

We the Jury on the issue
joined find the defendants
not guilty

J Fred Birrell
Foreman

9/15/27

STATE OF VIRGINIA,
CITY OF ALEXANDRIA. } TO-WIT: BE it remembered that on the _____ day of _____ 19__

of said city, came before me, Police Justice for said city, and severally and respectfully acknowledged themselves to
be indebted to the City of Alexandria, in the sum of _____
dollars, good and lawful money of the United States, to be respectfully made and levied on their several good and
chattels, lands and tenements, to the use of the city of Alexandria, if the said _____

of said city, at the next regular term thereof at ten o'clock a. m., and from time to time until this case is finally
disposed of, to answer the within charge, and shall be the meantime keep the peace and be of good behavior toward
_____ shall fail to personally appear before the Corporation Court

THE WITHIN NAMED _____ was brought before me this
_____ day of _____ 19__ and on the evidence of
_____ he is found
guilty of _____ as charged in the within Warrant, and I do adjudge
that he be confined in the jail of the City of Alexandria for _____ days, and pay a fine of
$ _____ and $ _____ cost.

Police Justice.

When the streetcar stopped in Alexandria, she told a police officer the boys would not give up their seats. George and Samuel were arrested. In court, they were found guilty of disorderly conduct.

Family friend and lawyer, Tom Watson, appealed the conviction. He argued that they were not disorderly. They had followed the rules. At their second trial, a jury of five white men found the boys not guilty. From this experience, Samuel Tucker learned that with evidence and convincing legal arguments, justice was sometimes possible in a court of law.

CHAPTER 5

Alexandria Library Sit-In, 1939

Anew public library was built in Alexandria in 1937. The library was only a block and a half from Samuel Tucker's house. But he could not use it because he was black. The library was for whites only.

He and a neighbor, retired U.S. Army Sergeant George Wilson, tried to get library cards at the new Alexandria Library. The librarian refused to give them cards. That irritated Tucker. So he decided he had to, "Do something about that."

As a student at Howard University, he learned about Mahatma Gandhi's successful nonviolent sit-in protests in India. He also knew about the autoworkers in Michigan who protested working conditions with a "sit-down strike." Lawyer Tucker decided to use this same strategy.

America's First Civil Rights Sit-In?

Autoworkers at the General Motors plant in Flint, Michigan, started a sit-down strike December 30, 1936. The strike was to protest working conditions. It lasted for 44 days.

The Alexandria Library sit-in protested civil rights violations. It was one of the earliest efforts to change laws through peaceful civil disobedience. In 1939, if not the first, it was certainly one of the first sit-ins of what would become the Civil Rights Movement.

Alexandria Library opened in 1937 at
717 Queen Street, Alexandria, Virginia.

Because they visited a city-supported library in
Alexandria, Va., these five young men were arrested last week and lodged in jail on charges of
disorderly conduct. They were, however, freed on
their own recognizance to await trial which has
been set for next Tuesday. Pictured as they were

being led away from the city library to the police
station are, left to right, William Evans, Otto L.
Tucker, Edward Gaddis, Morris L. Murray and
Clarence Strange. The policeman is Officer P.
Kelly.—Murray photo.

5 Arrested For Using City Library In Virginia; Case Puzzles Judge

ALEXANDRIA, Va., Sept. 1
—The Alexandria Jim-crow
library case took a different
turn this week when five
young men were arrested for
using the facilities of the city
library in what is considered by
observers a test case in the State
of Virginia.

With a case already pending in
the corporation court on the question of whether Race citizens have
the right to use the city-supported
library, municipal authorities were
again put to the test by the quintet.

The protesters, ages 18-22, being escorted from the Alexandria Library by Officer John F. Kelly on August 21, 1939. They were William (Buddy) Evans, Otto L. Tucker, Edward Gaddis, Morris Murray, and Clarence Strange.

He asked his younger brother Otto and ten other young men to protest the whites only policy at the Alexandria Library with a sit-in. They met several times in Tucker's law office to plan the protest. He assured them that if they followed his advice they would not go to jail.

On Monday morning, August 21, 1939, only six showed up—five protesters and one lookout. Some parents were worried and kept their sons home. One overslept. Some were scared, and only appeared later in the crowd outside the library.

As the protest began, Otto entered the library first and asked for a library card. About five minutes later, Morris Murray entered. He asked for a library card, too. The other three protesters each waited another five minutes. Then they, too, entered the library and asked for a library card. They were neatly dressed, polite, and orderly.

The white librarian refused to give the young men cards because they were black. Each protester took a book from a shelf and sat at a separate table. They read silently. They refused to leave. White people in the library stared, astounded. Nothing like this had ever happened before. The police were called.

The lookout, 14-year-old Bobby Strange, was outside watching. He ran the three blocks to Tucker's office to tell him the police were coming. Tucker had already called the newspapers. Reporters and photographers were on their way.

Officer Kelly politely advised the protesters that it would be better if they got up and left. Otto asked what would happen if they didn't leave. Kelly said they would be arrested. The protesters did not move. Morris said later he was so interested in the book he was reading that he did not want to stop reading. The young men put the books they were reading back on the shelves. Then the police arrested them.

News about the protest spread fast. When the police walked the protesters out of the library about two hours later, reporters, photographers, and around 300 people were outside watching. Alexandria and Washington newspapers reported the library "sit-down" strike. Newspapers as far as away as Pittsburgh, Chicago, and New York also carried the story.

The protestors were charged with "trespassing." Lawyer Tucker argued that it was a public library and these Alexandria citizens had just as much right to be there as anyone else. The judge agreed. The charge was changed to "disorderly conduct."

Lawyer Tucker defended the young men in court. During the hearing he asked, "Were they destroying property?"

"No," was the answer.

"Were they properly attired (dressed) for the library?"

"Yes," was the answer.

"Were they quiet?"

"Yes."

"Then they were disorderly only because they were black?" asked Tucker. The arresting officer and the librarian admitted this was true.

Judge Duncan delayed the case several times and, finally, made no ruling. The five protesters were not convicted. They never went to jail.

Interior of Alexandria Library about nine years after the sit-in.

More Southern "Jim-Crow".

Washington, D. C. — Alexandria, Va., opposite this city, is to open in April a new "jim-crow" branch of that little city's public library.

As reported in the *Cleveland* [Ohio] *Gazette* newspaper on March 30, 1940.

The Robert H. Robinson Library at 638 North Alfred Street in Alexandria, Virginia. It opened on April 24, 1940.

The library now is part of the Alexandria Black History Museum.

916 Queen Street

Alexandria, Virginia

February 13, 1940

Miss Katharine H. Scoggin, Librarian

Alexandria Library

Alexandria, Virginia

My dear Miss Scoggin:

Together with copy of letter from the City Manager
to you dated January 26, 1940, I am in receipt of your letter
of February 9 with reference to my application for library
privileges, filed January 30, 1940.

I refuse and will always refuse to accept a card to
be used at the library to be constructed and operated at Alfred
and Wythe Streets in lieu of card to be used at the existing
library on Queen Street for which I have made application.
Continued delay -- beyong the close of this month -- in issuing
to me a card for use at the library on Queen Street will be
taken as a refusal to do so, whereupon I will feel justified
in seeking the aid of court to enforce my right.

A letter is being sent to the City Manager on this
subject, a copy of which I am herewith enclosing.

Very truly yours,

SAMUEL WILBERT TUCKER

Alexandria quickly built a separate library for its black citizens. The new Robert Robinson Library opened less than a year after the sit-in. It cost half of what the library for whites cost to build. It was smaller and open fewer hours. The books were mostly old and the furniture was used. Its librarian was paid only half of what the city paid the white librarian.

Some in the black community were happy to have a library they could use. Tucker was disappointed and disgusted. This was not the victory he wanted. He wanted all Alexandria citizens to use the same library.

50   Military Service

CHAPTER 6

Military Service

While Samuel Tucker was at Howard University, he completed the Reserve Officers Training Corps (ROTC) program. He became a Second Lieutenant in the Infantry Reserve in July 1934. His leadership skills were noticed.

During the Great Depression, many young men worked in the Civilian Conservation Corps camps. The camps were segregated by race, but were run by white officers. In 1936, a new camp was formed at Gettysburg, Pennsylvania. This camp of black men had black Army Reserve officers. Tucker was asked to be one of the officers.

He accepted this assignment to

Civilian Conservation Corps (CCC)

During the Great Depression (1933-1939), people lost their jobs, farms, and businesses. Many people had no money to pay for food, clothes, and a place to live. President Franklin D. Roosevelt created the CCC to help. Unmarried, unemployed men, ages 18-25 who were U.S. citizens were hired to improve national parks and forests. They planted trees, and built roads and buildings. The pay was $30 a week. They had to send $25 a week home to their parents. The men were given housing, meals, and uniforms.

1st Lieutenant
S.W. Tucker

prove African Americans could be excellent officers and leaders. During his two years there, he had many jobs. He was a mess hall officer, motor transport officer, fire marshal, and construction officer. Skills he had learned in Mr. Ferguson's architectural drawing class in college were useful. He designed and helped build a recreation hall with a roof high enough to have a basketball court.

Tucker was called to active military duty in March 1941. The United States was preparing to enter World War II. He was an officer in the Army's all-black 366th Infantry Regiment. Other black units had white officers. The 366th had black soldiers and black officers.

After one year, Tucker was promoted to captain. He sailed for Europe in March 1944 aboard the USS *General William Mitchell*. The troop ship left Hampton Roads, Virginia, with about 3,000 soldiers aboard. It took ten days to get to Morocco in north Africa. The soldiers played cards to pass the time. Then, they went by train from Morocco to Algeria. They rode in boxcars that were 40 feet long and 8 feet wide, with only straw covering the floor. From Algeria, they went by ship across the Mediterranean Sea to Italy.

In Italy, Tucker's company guarded bombs and gasoline for airplanes. When soldiers had some free time, they went swimming in the ocean. Some soldiers became friends with Italian families and had dinners with them. Tucker went to operas and learned to like them.

When the 366th went into combat in December 1944, he was transferred to the 2nd Battalion Headquarters Company in a town in the mountains of northern Italy. He was the Executive Officer. His job was to make sure that soldiers were equipped, trained, and ready for battle. When the fighting was over and the war ended, Tucker thought, "some sort of greater power than I could imagine has spared me for something." He was honorably discharged from the army in March 1946.

Coming home after fighting for his country and still wearing his uniform, he was told he had to use the "colored" restroom in the Richmond, Virginia, bus station. He was ready to fight again for equal rights for African Americans back home.

USS *General William Mitchell* (AP-114) docked at Hampton Roads in 1944.

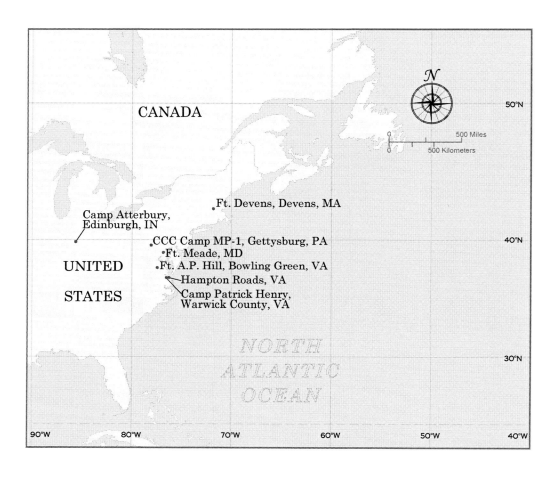

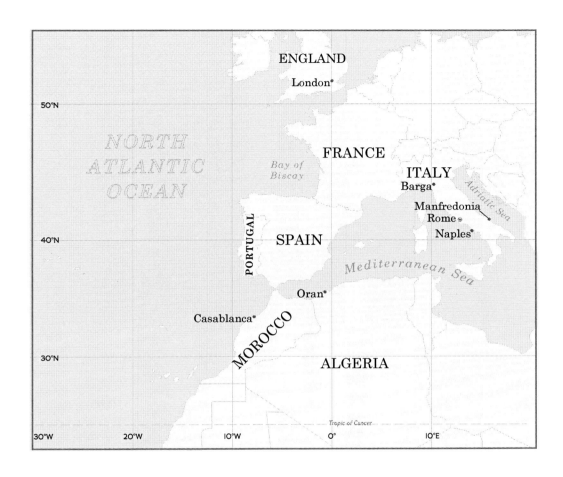

TUCKER'S MILITARY SERVICE TIMELINE

CCC Camp MP-1, Gettysburg, Pennsylvania
   Summer 1936 - Summer 1938.

Fort Devens, Devens, Massachusetts
   March 3, 1941: Joined 366th Infantry Regiment as a First Lieutenant.
      Assigned to the Officers Service Company as Personnel Officer.
      Responsible for records, orders, and payroll.
   April 23, 1942: Promoted to Captain.
   October 26, 1942: Transferred to Company C.
   March 28, 1943: Transferred to Headquarters Company, 2nd Battalion.
   September 4, 1943: Became Plans and Training Officer.
   October 13, 1943: Became S3 Training and Operations Officer.
      Scheduled and supervised training, planned troop movements, and
      was responsible for ammunition supply.

Fort A.P. Hill, Bowling Green, Virginia
   October 13, 1943–November 18, 1943.

Camp Atterbury, Edinburgh, Indiana
   November 18, 1943–March 21, 1944
   February 8, 1944: Assigned 2nd Battalion Executive Officer
   February 14, 1944: Assigned S1. Responsible for soldiers being
      equipped, trained, and healthy.

Camp Patrick Henry, Warwick County, Virginia
   March 21–27, 1944: Prepared to deploy to Europe.

Hampton Roads, Virginia
   March 28, 1944: Sailed from Hampton Roads, Virginia to Casablanca,
      Morocco on the USS *General William Mitchell* (AP-114). Entire
      366th Infantry Regiment was on board. Troop ship was unguarded

and unescorted. Soldiers slept below deck on stationary bunks stacked four high. Officers' quarters were above deck.

Casablanca, Morocco

April 6–19, 1944: Docked at Casablanca. Rode in train boxcars to Oran, Algeria. Boxcars were 40-feet long and 8-feet wide with no seats or restrooms. Floor covered with straw.

Oran, Algeria

April 19–30, 1944: Tucker became Commander of Cannon Company with 5 officers and 113 soldiers. Assigned guard duty. Sailed to Naples, Italy.

Naples, Italy

May 3–26, 1944: Arrived at Naples Staging Area. Rode in train and trucks to Manfredonia. Tucker reported that the Company ate C–rations for four days. (C–rations were canned meals. Each meal had a small can of meat with potatoes, vegetables or beans, and a can with bread and dessert. They were nutritious, easy to pack, and did not need refrigeration—but were not very tasty.)

Manfredonia, Italy

May 27, 1944: First day in Manfredonia. Went swimming in Adriatic Sea.

Cannon Company guarded an 8th Air Force Group airbase oil depot that had bombs and gasoline. Built a permanent mess hall for the company. Officers stayed in concrete bunkers, six officers to a bunker, and slept on cots.

November 23-27, 1944: Cannon Company relocated to camp near Barga.

Barga, Italy

November 1944–February 1945: 366th saw heavy fighting around Barga.

December 14, 1944: Tucker relieved as Commanding Officer of Cannon Company and transferred to 2nd Battalion Headquarters.

February 18, 1945: He became 2nd Battalion Headquarters Executive Officer.

March 8, 1945: 366th Infantry Regiment disbanded. Tucker assigned to 266th Engineer General Service Regiment responsible for building and repairing roads and bridges.

November 22, 1945: Returned to United States on Thanksgiving Day.

December 8, 1945: Tucker promoted to Major.

Fort Meade, Maryland, Separation Center

March 27, 1946: Tucker received honorable discharge from the U.S. Army.

COMPANY MORNING REPORT ENDING 2400 *27th May* 194*4*
(DAY) (MONTH) (YEAR)

STATION *Manfredonia, Italy*
ORGANIZATION *Cannon Co. 366th Inf.*
(CO. DET. ETC.) (PARENT UNIT) (ARM OR SERVICE)

SERIAL NUMBER	NAME	GRADE	CODE
	No change.		

OFFICER STRENGTH	FLD O & CAPT		1ST LT		2D LT		WO		FLT O	
	PRES	ABS'T	PRES	ABS'T	PRES	ABS'T	PRES	ABS'T	PRES	ABS'T
ASSIGNED	1		1		2					
ATTACHED UNASSIGNED										
ATTACHED FR OTHER ORGN										
TOTAL	1		1		2					

AVN CADET & ENLISTED STRENGTH	AVIATION CADETS		ENLISTED MEN			
	PRESENT	ABSENT	PRESENT FOR DUTY	PRESENT NOT FOR DUTY	ABSENT	PRESENT AND ABSENT
ASSIGNED			110		3	113
ATTACHED UNASSIGNED						
ATTACHED FR OTHER ORGN			24		1	25
TOTAL			134		4	138

RATIONS

I — ESTIMATED NUMBER OF RATIONS REQUIRED FOR — DAY OF WEEK *Wednesday* DATE *31st May 44* NUMBER *138*

II — MESS ATTENDANCE FOR DAY OF THIS REPORT
BREAKFAST *138* DINNER *138* SUPPER *138* TOTAL *414* ÷ 3 AVERAGE *138*

III — MEN ATTACHED TO MESS NOT RATIONED *0* MEN ATTACHED FOR RATIONS *0*
MEN ATTACHED TO OTHER ORGN FOR RATIONS *0* O B OTHERS MESSED *4*
MEN PRESENT *134* LESS *0* NET *134* PLUS *4* TOTAL *138*

PAGE *1* OF *1* PAGES

Samuel W. Tucker Capt. Inf.
SIGNATURE AND GRADE

Cannon Co. 366th Inf.
NAME

RECORD OF EVENTS

NO UNUSUAL EVENTS.
COMPANY USED ADRI-
ATIC FOR SWIMMING
FROM 1400 TO 1600.
WEATHER FAIR BUT
VERY WINDY.

Visiting Relatives

Tucker often visited his mother's family in Midland, Virginia. Aunt Maggie Williams was his mother's brother's wife. They lived near the farm where, as a young boy, Tucker had heard his grandfather talk about Jim Crow laws.

When Lawyer Tucker was working on a case in nearby Warrenton or Manassas, he could always count on Aunt Maggie to fix a delicious chicken dinner. Afterwards, the grownups sat on the porch. They talked and told stories.

When Tucker visited other relatives who had a piano, he would play and sing. The children were always happy when he visited because they got extra time to play outside. The children did not know about the important work Tucker was doing. They just knew he was family.

CHAPTER 7

Challenging School Segregation

Back home in Alexandria, Samuel Tucker decided to move his law practice to Emporia, Virginia. He worried that people in Alexandria would not take him seriously as a lawyer. They had known him since he was a child. They might still think of him as little Wilbert Tucker. Now he wanted to be known as Attorney S.W. Tucker.

Greensville County Courthouse in Emporia, Virginia, circa 1945.

In Emporia, he was the only black lawyer. African Americans there welcomed him. After he moved there, he married Julia E. Spaulding in 1947. Julia grew up in Newport News, Virginia. Their first home was an apartment above a movie theater.

They first met about ten years earlier when he helped a friend drive Julia's cousin from Alexandria to Newport News for a visit.

They met in the kitchen of her parents' home when he came in for a drink of water. When Tucker's army unit sailed for Europe, he asked Julia to write to him while he was gone. She did.

Julia graduated from West Virginia State College as a teacher. Before getting married, she taught school in Elkton, Maryland. Once she sent a student to the public library for a book. The student came back with no book. When she went to find out why, she said, "I realized there was no library this Negro child could go to."

In Emporia, Julia helped register African Americans to vote. People in Emporia said they welcomed her advice and encouragement "during those stressful days and turbulent years of our struggle" to desegregate the schools. The Tuckers loved children, but had none of their own. They shared the belief that reading meant freedom and that a good education led to opportunities.

In the 1950s, NAACP lawyers began to challenge "separate but equal" laws. They argued that separate schools for blacks had to be equal in every way to schools for whites. Thurgood Marshall, Oliver Hill, and Samuel Tucker were among the lawyers the NAACP recruited to challenge racial segregation.

Marshall led the team of lawyers (including Hill) that argued *Brown*

NAACP

The National Association for the Advancement of Colored People (NAACP) is the oldest and largest civil rights organization in the United States. It began in 1909. Members, both black and white, fought for social, economic, political, and educational equality.

The NAACP Legal Defense and Educational Fund began in 1940. Thurgood Marshall and other lawyers fought racial discrimination and segregation in courts of law. Today, the NAACP continues to fight for justice and equal treatment for all Americans.

v. The Board of Education of Topeka, Kansas. In 1954, the U.S. Supreme Court decided the case. All of the Supreme Court justices agreed that separate schools for black students and white students were not equal. They ruled that in public education "separate but equal has no place and is unconstitutional."

A year later, the Supreme Court looked at the *Brown* case again. The first ruling only declared that segregated schools were unconstitutional. In 1955, in what was called *Brown II*, the court ruled that school boards must desegregate schools "with all deliberate speed."

After the *Brown* decisions, school boards delayed desegregating public schools. In Virginia, Senator Harry F. Byrd led a government policy known as "massive resistance" to school desegregation. During the years of massive resistance, Tucker argued desegregation cases all over Virginia.

Laws were passed in Virginia to take state tax money away from schools that tried to integrate. Tax money was given to white students to go to private schools. Some schools closed rather than integrate. Public schools in Prince Edward County closed for five years. Tucker

> **Davis v. County School Board of Prince Edward County**
>
> One of the cases grouped with the *Brown* case was Oliver W. Hill's Virginia case, *Davis v. County School Board of Prince Edward County*. Sixteen-year-old Barbara Johns and other students at Moton High School in Farmville, Virginia, went on strike for 10 days. They were protesting terrible school conditions. Overcrowding put some classes in temporary buildings with tarpaper roofs. There were holes in the ceilings so students got wet when it rained. There was no gym or cafeteria. Not all students had desks. Classrooms had no chalkboards. Some classes met in school buses. The students walked out of school, but stayed on school grounds carrying picket signs demanding a better school. Hill agreed to take the case when the parents asked not just for a better school, but an integrated school.

Decision Is Blow To The Rights Of States – Byrd

Virginia's senior Senator, Harry F. Byrd, had the following to say of the Supreme Court's decision on segregation:

"The unanimous decision of the Supreme Court to abolish segre-...

**Independent Messenger
Emporia, Virginia
May 20, 1954**

...ates – Byrd

Virginia's senior Senator, Harry F. Byrd, had the following to say of the Supreme Court's decision on segregation:

"The unanimous decision of the Supreme Court to abolish segregation in public education is not only sweeping but will bring implications and dangers of the greatest consequence. It is the most serious blow that has been struck against the rights of the states in a matter vitally affecting their authority and welfare.

"The Supreme Court reversed its previous decision directing 'separate but equal' facilities for the education of both races. Nothing now remains for the Supreme Court to do except to determine the effective date and the method of the application of its decision.

"One of the cruel results arising out of this 'about-face' of the Supreme Court is that the Southern States, accepting the validity of the previous decision in recent years have expended hundreds of millions of dollars for construction of new Negro school facilities to conform with the policy previously laid down by the Court.

"Great progress has been made at tremendous cost throughout the Southern States to carry out that which our Southern State Governments had the right to believe was the law of the land. This reversal by the Supreme Court from its 'separate but equal' policy to complete abolition of segregation will create problems such as have never confronted us before.

"The decision will be deplored by millions of Americans, and, instead of promoting the education of our children, it is my belief that is will have the opposite effect in many areas of the country. In Virginia we are facing now a crisis of the first magnitude.

"Those in authority, and the parents directly affected in the education of their children, should exercise the greatest wisdom in shaping our future course.

"Whatever is done should be based on our most matured judgment after sober and exhaustive consideration."

helped reopen Prince Edward County schools in 1964. He argued it was not legal for the state to give white students money from public taxes to attend segregated private schools when black students had no public schools to attend.

In 1961, Tucker formed a law firm in Richmond with Henry L. Marsh, III. Marsh had recently finished law school. Tucker's friend Oliver Hill became a partner in Hill, Tucker and Marsh in 1966. In the 1960s, theirs was the leading black law firm handling desegregation cases in Virginia.

The Virginia State Bar was not pleased with the work NAACP lawyers were doing to desegregate public schools. Tucker was charged by the Virginia State Bar with "unethical" or improper professional

Thurgood Marshall

Thurgood Marshall was a graduate of the Howard University School of Law. He founded the NAACP's Legal Defense and Educational Fund. *Brown v. The Board of Education of Topeka, Kansas* was his landmark civil rights case. Marshall became a U.S. Supreme Court Justice in 1967. He was the first African American justice. Marshall was one of the justices who decided S.W. Tucker's case, *Green v. New Kent County.* Marshall served on the court 24 years, retiring in 1991.

Samuel W. Tucker

Oliver W. Hill

Henry L. Marsh, III

NAACP lawyers (left to right) Frank D. Reeves,
Henry L. Marsh, III, and Samuel W. Tucker in 1964.

conduct. They tried to take away his license to practice law. He fought the charges. It took two years and several times in court to prove the charges were false. They reprimanded (scolded) him, but did not take away his license. When it was over, hundreds of supporters celebrated with Tucker. School children gave him a trophy for his victory.

His 1968 U.S. Supreme Court case, *Green v. County School Board of New Kent County, Virginia,* did the most to speed up public school desegregation in America. School boards in Virginia began a "freedom of choice" integration plan. Students could decide themselves which school they would attend. The reality of freedom of choice, was that no white students chose to go to black public schools. Very few black students chose to face discrimination at white public schools. School boards used freedom of choice to keep public schools segregated.

People in rural New Kent County, Virginia, did not live in segregated areas. However, there were two separate schools, one for blacks and one for whites. The school board bused black students to the all-black school instead of the closer white school. Tucker argued that freedom of choice did not lead to desegregation. He said that under freedom of choice plans schools, students, faculty, transportation, and afterschool activities were still separate. In 1968, the Supreme Court agreed. In *Green,* the court ruled that school boards across America could no longer use freedom of choice as their desegregation plan. It forced school boards to show real progress. Now buses were used to intergrate schools.

Tucker was a lawyer for 50 years. He argued desegregation cases against more than 50 school boards in Virginia. Many of these cases

Royal Baptist Church, Emporia, Virginia

were complicated. They set precedents (standards) for future civil rights cases.

When he reflected on his cases' impacts on civil rights for African Americans, Tucker said he wasn't surprised about the *Brown* decision. Remembering his grandfather's comment about Jim Crow laws not always existing, he said he expected the Supreme Court to do what was right. What surprised him was that it took so long to put desegregation into practice. He said, "You must understand that the struggle to be free is paramount. You cannot suppress it without it taking over your heart." He considered the school desegregation cases part of "a continuous civil rights struggle."

CHAPTER 8

Tucker's Legacy

It took a long time and the work of many people to change segregation laws. Years later, S.W. Tucker said, "I got involved in the civil rights movement on June 18, 1913, in Alexandria, Virginia. I was born black."

In 1990 he had a heart attack and died in a Richmond hospital. He was 77 years old. Tucker is buried in Arlington National Cemetery. He had funeral services in Alexandria, Richmond, and Emporia. At his funeral in Emporia, a friend said, "Without Sam Tucker there would be no [Virginia] Governor Wilder and no [Richmond] Mayor Henry

**Samuel W. Tucker's gravestone
Arlington National Cemetery**

Marsh." Tucker ran for congress in Virginia two times. He did not win, but he wanted to give blacks a reason to get out and vote.

☒ VOTE FOR

S. W. TUCKER

(For Congressman from the Fourth Congressional District)

NOVEMBER 5, 1968

*A VOTE FOR TUCKER
IS A VOTE FOR FREEDOM*

Political Advertisement

Just like his father, Tucker worked to improve the lives of people in his community. Right after college he worked as a substitute teacher at Parker-Gray School. The Alexandria City Public Schools had started a night school for white adults. Tucker thought there should be a program for black adults, too. So he asked the superintendent of schools about this. The superintendent said he would get the money to pay teachers if Tucker would find them. He did. Tucker was happy his seventh grade teacher Henry T. White agreed to come out of retirement to teach grown ups.

He was a mentor to the young lawyers in his law firm. Five of them went on to become judges in Virginia. In 2001, the Virginia State Bar Association established the Oliver W. Hill–Samuel W. Tucker Scholarship. Scholarship recipients are first-year law students at Virginia law schools and Howard University.

Tucker did not want to be famous. He once said, "God keeps his eye on the sparrow, but the sparrow never shouts. He just sings

Civil Rights Movement, 1955-1972

Responding to a history of slavery, the Civil War, and separate but equal laws, African Americans and some white supporters organized peaceful actions to protest segregation and racial discrimination. They sat at lunch counters, boycotted buses, picketed stores, and marched to get equal treatment. The largest rally was the March on Washington in 1963 where Dr. Martin Luther King, Jr. gave his "I Have a Dream" speech.

Protests that began peacefully often ended violently as police broke up the demonstrations. Soldiers protected black students as they entered white schools. The National Association for the Advancement of Colored People (NAACP) led efforts to challenge segregation in courts of law.

Because of the Civil Rights Movement, laws were passed that improved how African Americans were treated. The 1954 *Brown v. Board of Education* case began the desegregation of public schools. The Civil Rights Act of 1964 made it illegal to discriminate against people because of race. The Voting Rights Act of 1965 said literacy tests and poll taxes could not be used to keep people from voting. The Civil Rights Act of 1968 made it illegal to discriminate by race against people buying, renting, or financing housing.

his song." Tucker was about 5'9" tall. He had a soft voice, and a thoughtful, planned way of speaking. He loved to tell stories and sometimes began them with the words, "This is a cute one." Some of the stories were surprising rather than funny.

Henry Marsh remembers, "Samuel Tucker lived civil rights and had little time to do anything else." He did stop and listen when operas were on the radio. He still loved to play the piano and autoharp.

Tucker never gave up hope. He understood that integration would take time. Desegregation had started the process. From the Alexandria Library sit-in in 1939 through the school desegregation

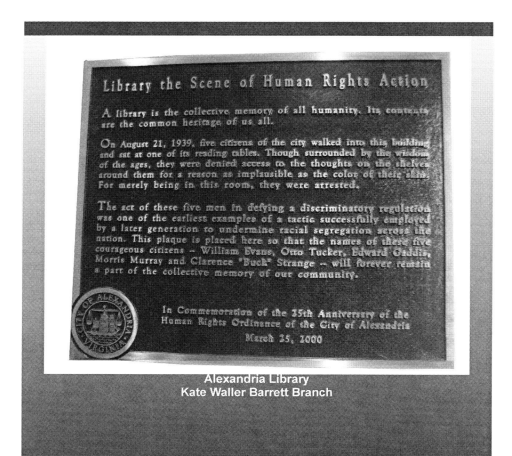

Alexandria Library
Kate Waller Barrett Branch

and civil rights cases he won, Samuel Wilbert Tucker was a civil rights trailblazer.

Today, we remember him for his determined, lifelong fight in the courts against discrimination and segregation. The NAACP Legal Defense and Educational Fund named him "Lawyer of the Year" in 1965.

A monument in Emporia honors him with the words, "He was an effective, unrelenting advocate for freedom, equality and human dignity, principles he loved—things that mattered."

The Robert Robinson Library closed in 1959. It is now part of the Alexandria Black History Museum. The museum's displays tell

ROBERT ROBINSON LIBRARY
1940

In the summer of 1939, Attorney Samuel W. Tucker organized six youths — William Evans, Otto Tucker, Edward Gaddis, Morris Murray, Clarence Strange and Robert Strange — for a "sit-in" at the segregated Alexandria Public Library, protesting the denial of access to the African American community. The "sit-in" is believed to have been the earliest in America. The arrest of five of these young men and their court case, pleaded by Mr. Tucker, resulted in a separate facility for African Americans being built here at 638 North Alfred Street, the present location of the Alexandria Black History Resource Center.

The Library is named after the Reverend Robert Robinson, a 19th century minister at the Roberts Chapel M.E. Church, in the 800 block of S. Washington Street. With Mrs. Evelyn Roper Beam as its first librarian, the Robert Robinson Library opened its doors to the African American community on April 24, 1940.

Alexandria Black History Museum

Above: Second from right, Elsie Tucker Thomas presents her brother S.W.'s portrait during the school's 2000 dedication ceremony.

the history of African Americans in and around Alexandria. Tucker's story is a part of that history.

After the Robinson Library closed, the Alexandria Library on Queen Street was integrated. Today a plaque in the library recognizes the 1939 sit-in. In 2009, third graders from Samuel W. Tucker Elementary School reenacted the sit-in at Alexandria Library's 70th anniversary event of the protest.

Samuel W. Tucker Elementary School was opened in 2000. It was named in honor of Tucker's work desegregating Virginia's public schools. On October 19, 2000 (the tenth anniversary of his death) the school was dedicated. Songs were sung. Speeches were given. Tucker's portrait was hung in the school's entrance. Students wrote about what his life and work meant to them, why he was a hometown hero. A fifth grader captured the spirit and legacy of this remarkable man in a poem titled "One Man of Many: Samuel W. Tucker's Struggle."

Samuel Wilbert Tucker fought for school desegregation and equality. He did not give up. He believed in the rule of law. As he looked back on how his court cases won civil rights, Tucker reflected, "We need to keep what progress we've made and keep fighting to get more." He added, "We've got to keep our story told."

One Man of Many
Samuel W. Tucker's Struggle

The history books and stories tell
Of men who fought for equal rights
Martin Luther King, Jr., Malcolm X
And Samuel W. Tucker joined in the fight.

He was not in search of public fame;
He just wanted to put segregation to shame.

This Virginia lawyer wanted equal rights for all free men,
And for those not receiving it-he would defend.

The sit-in at the library, the incident on the bus,
The hours in the courtroom;
Final victory for all of us.

It's Samuel Tucker's life song that I sing,
And we the people must continue to let freedom ring.

—**Taylor Sutton**

Taylor Sutton, Grade 5
Student Council President 2000
Samuel W. Tucker Elementary School

GLOSSARY

civil rights
>Personal rights, freedoms, and equal treatment guaranteed by the U.S. Constitution and the Bill of Rights.

desegregate/desegregation
>To end the separation of people by race.

discrimination
>The unfair treatment of people because of differences such as race.

integrate/integration
>To bring people together as equals in using public places like libraries, schools, restaurants, and buses.

segregate/segregation
>To separate people based on race.

sit-in
>An organized, non-violent occupation of a public place. Protesters refuse to leave to draw attention to a change they are demanding.

unconstitutional
>Not legal because it goes against something stated in the U.S. Constitution.

TIMELINE 1913-2000

1913   On June 18, Samuel Wilbert Tucker is born in Alexandria, VA.

1919   Samuel begins attending first grade.

1920   Samuel begins 2nd grade at Parker-Gray School.

1924   Samuel skips 5th grade and begins 6th grade.

1927   Samuel begins attending Armstrong High School in Washington, DC.

On June 21, George and Samuel Tucker are arrested for disorderly conduct on streetcar.

1929   On June 1, Samuel Tucker graduates from Armstrong High School.

In September, he begins college at Howard University in Washington, DC.

1933   In July, he graduates from Howard University.

In December, he takes and passes the Virginia State Bar exam.

1934   On June 18, he turns 21 years old.

On July 2, he is sworn in to practice law in Virginia.

In July, he joins the U.S. Army Reserve.

On December 27, he takes over Thomas Watson's law practice in Alexandria.

1936   On August 8, he is selected to be an officer at an all-black CCC camp.

1938   On September 30, he returns to Alexandria, VA, to practice law.

1939   On March 17, Tucker and Sergeant George Wilson apply for library cards at the Alexandria Library and are refused.

1939 On August 21, the peaceful sit-in organized by Tucker occurs at the Alexandria Library.

1940 On April 24, the Robert Robinson Library opens for Alexandria's black citizens.

1941 On March 3, Tucker begins active military duty in the 366th Infantry Regiment.

On December 7, Japanese planes bomb U.S. Navy ships in Pearl Harbor, HI. The United States declares war on Japan and joins World War II.

1941-1945 Tucker serves in the 366th Infantry Regiment, and then the 266th Engineer General Services Regiment. (See Chapter 6 in Military Service for details.)

1946 On March 27, he is honorably discharged from the U.S. Army. He moves to Emporia, VA, to practice law.

1947 On January 2, he marries Julia E. Spaulding. They live in Emporia.

On April 15, Jackie Robinson plays first base with the Brooklyn Dodgers, breaking the color barrier in major league baseball.

1954 On May 17, in the case of *Brown v. Board of Education of Topeka, Kansas (Brown I)* the U.S. Supreme Court rules public schools segregated by race are unconstitutional.

1955 On May 31, in the case of *Brown v. Board of Education (Brown II)* the U.S. Supreme Court rules that school boards need to desegregate schools "with all deliberate speed."

On December 1, Rosa Parks refuses to give up her seat on a Montgomery, AL, bus to a white man.

1960 Tucker also begins to practice law in Richmond, VA.

On February 1, four black students sit-in at a segregated Greensboro, NC, lunch counter. This led to similar nonviolent protests during the 1960s Civil Rights Movement.

1962 On February 15, a three-judge panel rejects the charges after a two-year effort to disbar Tucker.

1963 On August 28, Martin Luther King, Jr. leads the March on Washington and gives his "I have a dream" speech in front of the Lincoln Memorial.

1964 The Civil Rights Act of 1964 prohibits discrimination based on race, color, religion, or national origin.

In November, Tucker runs for Congress. He does not win.

1966 The law firm of Hill, Tucker and Marsh is established in Richmond, VA.

1968 On April 4, Martin Luther King, Jr., is assassinated in Memphis, TN.

On April 8, the Civil Rights Act of 1968 prohibiting discrimination in housing is signed.

On May 27, Tucker's U.S. Supreme Court case *Green v. County School Board of New Kent County* speeds up desegregation of public schools.

On November 5, he runs again for Congress. He does not win.

1971 The U.S. Supreme Court validates use of busing for school desegregation.

1990 On October 19, Tucker dies at age 77 in Richmond, Virginia. He is buried in Arlington National Cemetery.

1998 On June 21, the Samuel Wilbert Tucker Monument is dedicated in Emporia, VA.

2000 On September 5, Samuel W. Tucker Elementary School opens in Alexandria, VA.

On October 19, Samuel W. Tucker Elementary School is dedicated on the 10th anniversary of his death.

TO LEARN MORE

BIOGRAPHIES

School and public libraries have biographies of Thurgood Marshall, Rosa Parks, Ruby Bridges, Martin Luther King, Jr., Malcolm X, Jesse Owens, Marian Anderson, Jackie Robinson, Althea Gibson, Arthur Ashe, and other Civil Rights trailblazers.

NONFICTION

McKissack, Patricia, and Fredrick McKissack. *The Civil Rights Movement in America: From 1865 to the Present.* Chicago, IL: Children's Press, 1991. Detailed history of the struggle of African Americans for fair treatment and equal opportunities. Includes Reconstruction, segregation, protests, marches, sit-ins, legal challenges, and the Civil Rights Acts of the 1960s.

Osborne, Linda Barrett. *Miles to Go for Freedom: Segregation & Civil Rights in the Jim Crow Years.* New York, NY: Abrams Books for Young Readers, 2012. Photographs and interviews tell the daily experiences of African Americans from the late 1800s through the mid-1950s.

Pinkney, Andrea Davis. *Sit-In: How Four Friends Stood Up by Sitting Down.* New York, NY: Little, Brown, 2010. A celebration of the 50th anniversary of the Woolworth's lunch counter sit-in February 1, 1960.

Rappaport, Doreen. *The School is Not White! A True Story of the Civil Rights Movement.* New York, NY: Hyperion Books for Children, 2005. The Carters, a sharecropper family in Mississippi, sent their children to an all-white school in 1965. There they faced the racism of white children, adults, and teachers in their fight for an equal education and opportunities.

Shelton, Paula Young. *Child of the Civil Rights Movement.* New York, NY: Schwartz & Wade Books, 2010. Daughter of civil rights leader Andrew Young tells of the march from Selma to Montgomery, Alabama, in the early days of the movement. Leaders like Martin Luther King, Jr. were family friends.

HISTORICAL FICTION

McKissack, Patricia. *Abby Takes a Stand.* New York, NY: Viking, 2005. Gee tells about passing out fliers in Nashville, Tennessee while her cousin participates in a sit-in to protest segregation.

Ramsey, Calvin Alexander. *Ruth and the Green Book.* Minneapolis, MN: Carolrhoda Books, 2010. Ruth and her parents drive from Chicago to Alabama. A guidebook called "The Negro Motorist Green Book" helps them find places that serve African Americans.

Reynolds, Aaron. *Back of the Bus.* New York, NY: Philomel Books, 2009. A young boy sitting in the back of the bus with his mother watches Rosa Parks refuse to give up her seat.

Weatherford, Carole Boston. *Freedom on the Menu: The Greensboro Sit-Ins.* New York, NY: Dial Books for Young Readers, 2004. The Woolworth lunch counter sit-in seen through the eyes of a young black girl.

Wiles, Deborah. *Freedom Summer.* New York, NY: Atheneum Books for Young Readers, 2001. A Mississippi town fills its swimming pool with tar rather than integrate it after the Civil Rights Act of 1964. Best friends, one black and one white, learn that a law does not eliminate racism.

Woodson, Jacqueline. *The Other Side.* New York, NY: Putnam Juvenile, 2001. A friendship between Clover and Anna grows in a town where a fence separates the races.

SONGS

Johnson, James Weldon. *Lift Every Voice and Sing.* New York, NY: Amistad, 2007. An illustrated version of what is known as the African American national anthem.

WEB SITES

Alexandria Black History Museum, 902 Wythe Street, Alexandria, VA

HTTP://ALEXANDRIAVA.GOV/BLACKHISTORY

Alexandria Library, Kate Waller Barrett Branch, 717 Queen Street, Alexandria, VA

HTTP://WWW.ALEXANDRIA.LIB.VA.US

Alexandria Archaeology Museum, 105 North Union Street, #327, Alexandria, VA

HTTP://ALEXANDRIAVA.GOV/ARCHAEOLOGY

Samuel W. Tucker Elementary School, 435 Ferdinand Day Drive, Alexandria, VA

HTTP://WWW.ACPS.K12.VA.US/TUCKER/INDEX.PHP

SOURCE NOTES

These notes identify the sources of information, stories, and quotations in each chapter.

Chapter 1 – Early Life and Family

U.S. Census records (1900, 1910, 1920, 1930,1940) for the Tucker and Williams families.

Alexandria City Directory records for the Tucker family. *(Richmond's Directory of Alexandria,* VA, 1900, 1903, 1907; *Alexandria City Directory*, 1910, 1915; *Boyd's Directory of Alexandria,* VA, 1917; *Hill's Alexandria City Directory,* 1924, 1932, 1934, 1936, 1938,1940.

Pages 13-17   *Interview with Samuel Wilbert Tucker,* January 17, 1985. Parts 2 and 3.

Page 14   Samuel A. Tucker, Jr. report card, Alexandria Black History Museum.

Page 14   *Interview with Elsie Thomas,* April 21, 2002.

Page 17   *Interview with Julia Tucker and Oliver W. Hill,* February 28, 1995.

Page 17   **"to stand on my feet and say what needs to be said."** *Interview with Samuel Wilbert Tucker,* January 17, 1985, Part 3.

Chapter 2 – Queen Street Neighborhood

Information for this chapter came from the Alexandria City Directories (*Richmond's Directory of Alexandria,* VA, 1900, 1903, 1907; *Alexandria City Directory,* 1910, 1915; *Boyd's Directory of Alexandria,* VA, 1917; *Hill's Alexandria City Directory* 1924, 1932, 1934, 1936, 1938,1940); The Uptown Parker-Gray Historic District application; *Out of Obscurity: The Story of the 1939 Alexandria Library Sit-In;* and interviews with Samuel Tucker and Elsie [Tucker] Thomas.

Page 19　　　*Rise and Fall of Jim Crow. Jim Crow Stories.* http://www.pbs.org/wnet/jimcrow/stories_events_plessy. html. Accessed April 17, 2013; *Who was Jim Crow.* http:// www.ferris.edu/jimcrow/who.htm. Accessed May 13, 2013.

Pages 19-25　*Uptown/Parker-Gray Historic District.* http://alexandriava.gov/planning/info/default.aspx?i d=10190&terms=uptown+neighborhood. Accessed August 13, 2013; *Interview with Elsie Thomas,* April 21, 2002.

Page 23　　　**"When my mother was very sick, Mrs. Duncan would come and bring food, or find out if there was anything she could do to help,"** *Interview with Elsie Thomas,* April 21, 2002.

Page 23　　　**"my little world"** *Interview with Samuel Wilbert Tucker and Otto L. Tucker,* January 18, 1985, Part 2.

Chapter 3 – School Days

Page 26   *A History of Negro Education in the Alexandria City Public Schools 1900-1964; The Parker-Gray Story.* Vertical File, Alexandria Black History Museum.

Pages 27-30   *Interview with Samuel Wilbert Tucker,* January 17, 1985, Part 3 and May 25, 1985, Part 1.

Page 29   *Bison* Yearbook 1933, 36-37.

Page 30   *Interview with Julia Tucker and Oliver W. Hill,* February 28, 1995, 17; *Conversations with Civil Rights Crusaders Oliver Hill and Samuel Tucker,* February 1989, 39.

Page 31   *Interview with Elsie Thomas,* September 30, 1998; *Interview with Henry L. Marsh III,* May 24, 2013.

Chapter 4 – Experiences Shape the Man

Page 33   **Samuel A. Tucker Jr.** **"We've fought every race's battle, but our own…fighting till we set our own race free," "Always ready for battle when there's fighting work to do."** *Interview with Samuel Wilbert Tucker,* January 17, 1985, Part 1; *Interview with Samuel Wilbert Tucker and Otto L. Tucker,* January 18, 1985, Part 1.

Page 35   **G. David Williams "That was before they Jim Crowed us."** *Interview with Samuel Wilbert Tucker,* January 17, 1985, Part 1.

Pages 35-36   **Thomas Watson** *Interview with Samuel Wilbert Tucker,*

January 17, 1985, Part 3; **"grew up in that law office like a kid with two fathers, each one expecting me to take over their business."** *Conversations with Civil Rights Crusaders,* 38.

Page 36   **Rozier D. Lyles** *Interview with Samuel Wilbert Tucker,* January 17, 1985, Part 3.

Pages 36-38   **Discrimination** *Interview with Julia Tucker,* November 21, 1998; *Interview with Samuel Wilbert Tucker and Otto L. Tucker,* January 18, 1985, Part 1; *City of Alexandria v. Geo Tucker and Wm Tucker,* September 15, 1927.

Chapter 5 – Alexandria Library Sit-in, 1939

Pages 41-49   *Interview with Samuel Wilbert Tucker and Otto L. Tucker,* January 18, 1985. Parts 2 and 3; "5 Arrested at City Library," *Alexandria Gazette,* August 21, 1939, 1; "Five Colored Youths Stage Alexandria Library 'Sit-Down,'" *Washington Post,* August 22, 1939, 3; "Quintet Arrested for Library 'Sit-Down,'" *Washington Tribune,* August 26, 1939, 7; 5 "Youths Face Strike Charge," *New York New Amsterdam,* September 9, 1939, 3; *Managing White Supremacy: Race, Politics, and Citizenship in Jim Crow Virginia,* 259-270.

Page 41   http://www.history.com/this-day-in-history/sit-down-strike-begins-in-flint. Accessed May 13, 2013; **"... decided to do something about that,"** *Interview with Samuel Wilbert Tucker and Otto L. Tucker,* January 18, 1985, Part 2.

Page 44   *Interview with Ferdinand Day,* January 17, 2012.

Page 45   "5 Arrested for Using City Library in Virginia; Case
                 Puzzles Judge," *Chicago Defender,* September 2,
                 1939, 1; *Interview with William Evans,* January 18,
                 1985; "Reading as a Black-and-White Fight," *Arlington
                 Journal,* December 6, 1990, 1.

Page 47   "Judicial Red Tape Delays Library Case*," Chicago
                 Defender,* September 9, 1939, 6; "More Southern 'Jim
                 Crow,'" *Cleveland Gazette,*   March 30, 1940; "New
                 Colored Library Branch to Open to Public Tomorrow,"
                 Alexandria Gazette, April 22, 1940.

Page 48   *Tucker letter to Katharine H. Scoggin,* February 13,
                 1940.

Chapter 6 – Military Service

Pages 51-52   *Bison* Yearbook, 1933, *Record of 1st Lieutenant
                 Samuel Wilbert Tucker,* 86.

Pages 51-53   *Interview with Samuel Wilbert Tucker and Otto L.
                 Tucker,* January 18, 1985, Part 2; *Interview with
                 Samuel Wilbert Tucker,* May 25, 1985, Part 1; *This
                 is your life Samuel Wilbert Tucker,* June 17, 1979;
                 Samuel Tucker Interview at Reunion of 366th, 1981,
                 88-89.

Page 53   **"...some sort of greater power than I could
                 imagine has spared me for something."** "25 Years
                 After Brown: Tucker Recalls Battle Over Integration,"

Richmond Times Dispatch, May 13, 1979, 3; Discharge certificate March 27, 1946, Vertical file, Alexandria Black History Museum; *Interview with Oliver W. Hill and Samuel Wilbert Tucker,* October 26, 1985, Part 2.

Pages 56-59   Email from James Pratt, April 10, 2013; *Interview with Frank Cloud,* April 13, 2013.

Chapter 7 – Challenging School Segregation

Page 60   *Interviews with Sandra Slaughter,* June 27, 2013 and August 5, 2013.

Pages 61-69   *Interview with Samuel Wilbert Tucker,* January 17, 1985, Part 3; "25 Years After Brown: Tucker Recalls Battle Over Integration," *Richmond Times Dispatch,* May 13, 1979, 1 and 3; *Interview with Julia Tucker,* November 21, 1998; *Greensville County's Memorial Tribute to Attorney S.W. Tucker,* October 26, 1990; *Interview with Julia Tucker and Oliver W. Hill,* February 28, 1995.

Page 62   **"I realized there was no library this Negro child could go to."** *Interview with Julia Tucker,* November 21, 1998; **"...during those stressful days and turbulent years of our struggle..."** *Greensville County's Memorial Tribute to Attorney S.W. Tucker,* October 26, 1990.

Page 62   *NAACP Legal History,* NAACP. http://www.naacp. org/pages/naacp-legal-history. Accessed May 13, 2013; *Civil Rights Movement (1955-1972)* http://www.

nps.gov/brvb/historyculture/civilrights.htm. Accessed May 13, 2013; *NAACP Legal Defense Fund: Defend, Educate, Empower.* http://www.naacpldr.org/history. Accessed May 16, 2013.

Page 63 **"...separate but equal has no place and is unconstitutional."** http://www.nationalcenter.org/brown.html. Accessed May 16, 2013; **"...with all deliberate speed."** http://www.nationalcenter.org/cc0725.htm. Accessed May 16, 2013; "Brown Case - Davis v. Prince Edward County." *Brown Foundation.* March 14, 2013; *Black Students on Strike! Farmville, Virginia.* http://americanhistory.si.edu/brown/history/4-five/farmville-virginia-1.html. Accessed April 22, 2013; *Desegregation in Public Schools.* http://www.encyclopediavirginia.org/Desegregation_in_Public_Schools#start_entry. Accessed April 22, 2012.

Pages 63-64 *Massive Resistance. "The Civil Rights Movement in Virginia."* www.vahistorical.org/civilrights/massiveresistance.htm. Accessed March 13, 2012; *Independent Messenger,* May 20, 1954.

Page 65 *Thurgood Marshall* http://www.biography.com/people/thurgood-marshall-9400241. Accessed May 15, 2013.

Pages 65-67 *Interview with Henry L. Marsh III,* May 24, 2013; Virginia: in the Circuit Court of the County of Greensville; In the Matter of Complaint against S.W. Tucker, An Attorney at Law, February 15, 1962; "Va. Court Drops Charges Against NAACP Attorney: Reprimand Given In Another Case," *Baltimore Afro-American,* February 3, 1962 and *Richmond Afro-American,* February 15, 1962.

Page 67   *Interview with Samuel Wilbert Tucker,* May 25, 1985, Part 2; *Charles C. Green et. al. v. County School Board of New Kent County.* http://www.encyclopediavirginia.org/Green_Charles_C_et_al_v_County_School_Board_of_New_Kent_County_Virginia **Accessed** April 22, 2013; *Conversations with Civil Rights Crusaders Oliver Hill and Samuel Tucker,* 37-41; *New Kent School and the George W. Watkins School: From Freedom of Choice to Integration.* http://www.nps.gov/nr/twhp/wwwlps/lessons/104newkent/104facts1.htm. Accessed July 23, 2013.

Page 69   *Interview with Samuel Wilbert Tucker and Otto L. Tucker,* January 18, 1985, Parts 1, 4 and 5; **"You must understand that the struggle to be free is paramount. You can not suppress it without it taking over your heart."** "One Brave Soldier in the Fight To Be Free," *Washington Post,* November 11, 1990; **"...a continuous civil rights struggle."** **"25 Years After Brown: Tucker Recalls Battle Over Integration,"** *Richmond Times Dispatch,* May 13, 1979, 1.

Chapter 8 – Tucker's Legacy

Page 71   **"I got involved in the civil rights movement..."** *A* "Tribute to S.W. Tucker: NAACP Lawyer Who Beat Massive Resistance," *Richmond Free Press,* February 18-20, 1993; "Samuel Tucker, 77, Civil Rights Lawyer, Dies, October 21, 1990;" "One Brave Soldier in the Fight To Be Free," *Washington Post,* November 11, 1990.

Page 72   **"God keeps his eye on the sparrow, but the sparrow never shouts. He just sings his song."** *Samuel Wilbert Tucker: The Unsung Hero of the School Desegregation Movement,* 2000.

Page 72 & 74 *Interview with Henry L. Marsh III,* May 24, 2013; *Interview with Samuel Wilbert Tucker,* January 17, 1985, Parts 1 and 3; *Tribute to Samuel W. Tucker,* Alexandria Black History Museum, May 20, 1991; *Interview with Elsie Thomas,* September 30, 1998; *This is your life Samuel Wilbert Tucker,* June 16, 1979.

Page 73   *NAACP Legal History*, NAACP. http://www.naacp.org/pages/naacp-legal-history. Accessed May 13, 2013; *Civil Rights Movement (1955-1972)* http://www.nps.gov/brvb/historyculture/civilrights.htm. Accessed May 13, 2013.

Page 74   **"This is a cute one."** "25 Years After Brown: Tucker Recalls Battle Over Integration," *Richmond Times Dispatch,* May 13, 1979, 1; **"Samuel Tucker lived civil rights and had little time to do anything else."** *Interview with Henry L. Marsh III,* November 5, 1998.

Page 75   *Tribute to Samuel W. Tucker,* May 20, 1991; *In Celebration of the Life of Samuel Wilbert Tucker,* October 26, 1990; **"He was an effective, unrelenting advocate for freedom, equality and human dignity, principles he loved—things that mattered."** Monument to Samuel Wilbert Tucker, Emporia, VA.

Pages 76-78   "Shhh! History Being Made," *Alexandria Gazette,* 1; "Samuel Tucker Students Remember Library

98

Sit-In," *Alexandria News,* August 21, 2009. http://alexandrianews.org/2009/schools/samuel-tucker-students-remember-library-sit in/7331. Accessed May 19, 2013; *Third Graders and Local History.* August 24, 2009. http://teachinghistory.org/nhec-blog/22515. Accessed March 26, 2013; *Dedication of Samuel W. Tucker Elementary School* Program, October 19, 2000; *One Man of Many: Samuel W. Tucker's Struggle.* 2000; ***"We need to keep what progress we've made and keep fighting to get more...We've got to keep our story told."*** *Interview with Samuel Wilbert Tucker and Otto L. Tucker,* January 18, 1985, Part 5.

BIBLIOGRAPHY

Alexandria Black History Museum's vertical files have newspaper articles, original research, letters, and photographs organized by topic: Samuel W. Tucker, 1939 Library Sit-in, and Elsie Tucker Thomas. Special Collections at Alexandria Library's Kate Waller Barrett Branch has vertical files with folders for Samuel Tucker and the Alexandria Library Sit-Down Strike.

Ackerman, S.J. "Samuel Wilbert Tucker: The Unsung Hero of the School Desegregation Movement." *The Journal of Blacks in Higher Education,* 2000.

Ackerman, S.J. Telephone interview by author, December 15, 2012.

Ackerman, S.J. E-mail correspondence with author, May 26, 2013.

Alexandria City Directory. 1910.

Allen, Jody, and Brian J. Daugherity. *Charles C. Green et. al. v. County School Board of New Kent County.* Encyclopedia of Virginia. http://www.encyclopediavirginia.org/Green_Charles_C_et_al_v_County_School_Board_of_New_Kent_County_Virginia Accessed April 22, 2013.

Army of the United States. Discharge certificate for Samuel W. Tucker, March 27, 1946.

Benton, James W., Jr. "Tribute to Samuel W. Tucker." Letter to Alexandria Black Resource Center. May 20, 1991.

Bison Yearbook. Howard University, 1933.

"Black Students on Strike! Farmville, Virginia." Smithsonian National Museum of American History. http://americanhistory.si.edu/brown/history/4-five/farmville-virginia-1.html Accessed April 22, 2013.

Boyd's Directory of Alexandria, VA., 1917: Containing a General Directory of Alexandria, New Alexandria, West End, Seminary Heights, Rosemont, Braddock Heights, Mt. Ida, Del Ray, Hume, Potomac, Aurora Hills, Virginia Highlands and South Washington; Together with a Complete Business Directory; Also the State and City Governments, Secret and Other Orders, Churches Etc. Washington, DC: Boyd's Directory, 1917.

Branch, Carla, and James Cullum. "Samuel Tucker Students Remember Library Sit-In." *Alexandria News,* August 21, 2009. http://alexandrianews.org/2009/schools/samuel-tucker-students-remember-library-sit-in/7331/ Accessed March 13, 2013.

"Brown Case–Davis v. Prince Edward County." http://brownvboard.org/content/brown-case-davis-v-prince-edward-county Accessed March 14, 2013.

"Civil Rights: *Brown v. Board of Education I*" May 17, 1954. http://www.
   nationalcenter.org/brown.html Accessed May 16, 2013.

"Civil Rights: *Brown v. Board of Education II*" May 31, 1955. http://www.
   nationalcenter.org/cc0725.htm Accessed May 16, 2013.

"City of Alexandria v. Geo Tucker and Wm Tucker." Arrest Warrant,
   September 15, 1927.

"Civilian Conservation Corps (CCC)" http://www.u-s-history.com/pages/
   h1586.html Accessed May 14, 2013.

Cloud, Frank. Telephone interview by author, April 13, 2013.

Day, Ferdinand. Personal interview by author, January 17, 2012.

Daugherity, Brian J. "Desegregation in Public Schools." *Encyclopedia
   Virginia,* http://www.encyclopediavirginia.org/Desegregation_in_Public_
   Schools Accessed March 13, 2013.

Daugherity, Brian J., and Jody Allen. *"Charles C. Green et. al. v. County
   School Board of New Kent County, Virginia." Encyclopedia Virginia*
   http://www.encyclopediavirginia.org/Green_Charles_C_et_al_v_
   County_School_Board_of_New_Kent_County_Virginia Accessed March
   13, 2013.

"Dedication of Samuel W. Tucker Elementary School, October 19, 2000."
   Program.

Dolan, Laurel. *A History of Negro Education in the Alexandria City
   Public Schools 1900-1964.* Unpublished manuscript, 1969. Special
   Collections, Alexandria Library, Alexandria, Virginia.

Evans, William (Buddy) personal interview by William A. Elwood. January
   18, 1985. University of Virginia Library, Charlottesville, VA. http://search.
   lib.virginia.edu/catalog/r009

*Encyclopedia of African American History 1619-1895: From the Colonial
   Period to the Age of Frederick Douglass,* New York, NY: Oxford
   University Press, 2006.

"Green v. County School Board of New Kent County." *Green v. County
   School Board of New Kent County.* http://www.law.cornell.edu/supct/
   html/historics/USSC_CR_0391_0430_ZO.html Accessed March 13,
   2013.

"Greensville County's Memorial Tribute to S.W. Tucker," Greensville County
   Branch NAACP, October 26, 1990. Vertical File, Alexandria Black
   History Museum.

Higgenbotham, A. Leon. "Conversations with Civil Rights Crusaders Oliver
   Hill and Samuel Tucker." *Virginia Lawyer,* February 1989.

Hill's Alexandria (Virginia) City Directory. Richmond, VA: Hill Directory, 1924, 1932, 1934, 1936, 1938, and 1940.

Hill, Oliver W, and Samuel Wilbert Tucker personal interviews by William Elwood, October 26, 1985. *Special Collections, University of Virginia Library* http://search.lib.virginia.edu/catalog/u5366345

"A History Lesson at the Library." *Washington Post,* August 27, 2009.

"In Celebration of the Life of Samuel Wilbert Tucker June 18, 1913-October 19, 1990." Funeral Program.

Kopf, Curtis. "Reading as Black and White Fight: Pioneer Sit-In Is Recalled." *Arlington* [VA] *Journal,* December 6, 1990, A1 and A3.

Marsh, III, Henry L. Personal interview by Matt Spangler, November 5, 1998.

Marsh, III, Henry L. Telephone interview by author, May 24, 2013.

Marshall, Thurgood. http://www.biography.com/people/thurgood-marshall-9400241 Accessed May 15, 2013; "Massive Resistance." *Virginia Historical Society,* March 13, 2012.

"NAACP." http://www.naacp.org/ Accessed May 16, 2013.

"New Kent School and the George W. Watkins School: From Freedom of Choice to Integration." http://www.nps.gov/nr/twhp/wwwlps/lessons/104newkent/104facts1.htm Accessed July 23, 2013.

"Oliver W. Hill Sr. Memorial Service." Howard University. September 7, 2007.

"Parker-Gray History." http://alexandriava.gov/recreation/info/default.aspx?id=24578#Parker-GrayHistory Accessed August 12, 2013.

"The Parker-Gray Story." Vertical file, Alexandria Black History Museum, Alexandria, VA.

Pictorial History 366th Infantry, United States Army, Fort Devens, MA. *Officers Service Company* and *Record of 1st Lieutenant Samuel Wilbert Tucker,* 1941.

Pratt, James. E-mail correspondence with author, April 10, 2013.

Richmond's Directory of Alexandria, Virginia. Richmond, VA: 1900, 1903, and 1907.

The Rise and Fall of Jim Crow. Jim Crow Stories. Educational Broadcasting Corporation. http://www.pbs.org/wnet/jimcrow/stories_events_plessy.html Accessed April 17, 2013.

"Samuel Wilbert Tucker Collections," M56, Special Collections and Archives, James Branch Cabell Library, Virginia Commonwealth University, Richmond, VA.

"Samuel Wilbert Tucker: Major, United States Army." www.

arlingtoncemetery.net/swtucker.htm Accessed November 6, 2011.

Samuel Wilbert Tucker to Katharine H. Scoggin, February 13, 1940. Special Collections, Alexandria Library.

"Sit-Down Strike Begins in Flint". http://www.history.com/this-day-in-history/sit-down-strike-begins-in-flint Accessed May 13, 2013.

Slaughter, Sandra. Personal interviews by author, June, 27, 2013 and August 5, 2013.

Smith, J. Douglas. *Managing White Supremacy: Race, Politics, and Citizenship in Jim Crow Virginia.* Chapel Hill, NC: University of North Carolina Press, 2001.

Spangler, Matt. *Out of Obscurity: The Story of the 1939 Alexandria Library Sit-In*, VHS. River Road Productions, 1999.

Sutton, Taylor. "One Man of Many: Samuel W. Tucker's Struggle." Poem, 2000.

This is Your Life: Samuel Wilbert Tucker. Program. Sponsored by the Youth Councils of National Association for the Advancement of Colored People, Virginia State College, June 16, 1979.

Thomas, Elsie (Tucker). Personal interview by Matt Spangler, September 30, 1998.

Thomas, Elsie (Tucker). Personal interview, April 21, 2002; transcribed by Valerie Davison. Alexandria Legacies Oral History Project, City of Alexandria/Office of Historic Alexandria. Tape Repository at the Alexandria Archaeology Museum. http://alexandriava.gov/uploadedFiles/historic/info/history/OHAOralHistoryThomas2002.pdf

Thomas, Elsie (Tucker). Personal interview by Donise Stevens, December 15, 2006. Alexandria Legacies Oral History Project, City of Alexandria/Office of Historic Alexandria. http://alexandriava.gov/uploadedFiles/historic/info/history/OHAOralHistoryThomas2006.pdf

Tucker, Julia (Spaulding). Personal interview by Matt Spangler, November 21, 1998.

Tucker, Julia (Spaulding). Personal interview by John H. Whaley, February 28, 1995. Virginia Commonwealth University, Richmond, VA.

Tucker, Samuel Wilbert. Arlington National Cemetery burial. http://public.mapper.army.mil/ANC/ANCWeb/PublicWMV/ancWeb.html

Tucker, Otto L. Personal interview by William A. Elwood, January 18, 1985. University of Virginia, Charlottesville, VA. http://search.lib.virginia.edu/catalog/r008

Tucker, Samuel Wilbert. Personal interview by William Elwood, January 17,

1985. University of Virginia. http://search.lib.virginia.edu/catalog/r007 and http://search.lib.virginia.edu/catalog/r008

Tucker, Samuel Wilbert. Personal interview by Judge A. Leon Higgenbotham, May 25, 1985. University of Virginia. http://search.lib.virginia.edu/catalog/r013

Tucker, Samuel Wilbert. Personal interview by William Elwood, October 26, 1985. University of Virginia. http://search.lib.virginia.edu/catalog/u5366345

Tucker, Samuel Wilbert. Interview at 366th's 40th Reunion. Howard University, 1981.

United States Population Census, 1900, 1920, 1930.

Uptown Parker-Gray Historic District. Alexandria Planning & Zoning Department. http://alexandriava.gov/uploadedFiles/planning/info/pnz_parkergrayinfoform.pdf

Virginia: In the Circuit Court of the County of Greensville; In the Matter of Complaint against S.W. Tucker, An Attorney at Law, February 15, 1962.

Who was Jim Crow? http://www.ferris.edu/jimcrow/who.htm Accessed May 13, 2013.

ILLUSTRATION CREDITS

Afro-American—Page 68 (upper)

Alexandria Black History Museum—Front Cover; Pages 14, 26, 27, 36, and 47 (lower)

Alexandria Library, Special Collections—Pages 25, 42, 46, and 48

Army Press—Page 52

Chicago [IL] *Defender*—Pages 1, 42, 43, and 112

Cleveland [OH] *Gazette*—Page 47 (upper)

Franklin D. Roosevelt Presidential Library and Museum—Page 58

Henry L. Marsh, III—Page 66 (portraits)

Howard University—Page 29

Independent Messenger [Emporia, VA]—Page 64

James Pratt—Page 59

Library of Congress—Pages 18, 39, 65, 69, and 73

Lillian Patterson—Page 25

Nancy Noyes Silcox—Pages 13, 15, 20, 21, 22, 23, 37, 71, 74, 75, and 76 (lower)

NavSource.org—Pages 53 and 57

Richmond [VA] *Times-Dispatch*—Page 66 (lower)

Royal Baptist Church, Emporia—Page 68 (lower)

Sandra Slaughter—Pages 60 and 76 (upper and middle)

Shutterstock—Pages 16 and 34

Taylor Sutton—Page 78

The Library of Virginia—Page 61

University of Virginia—Pages 30, 33, and 79; Back Cover

Virginia Commonwealth University—Page 72

Yvonne Narcisse Green—Page 107

ACKNOWLEDGMENTS

Many people, who were generous with their advice and comments, helped this book become a reality. Third grade students in Lynda Gallagher and Jackie Swift's classes at Samuel W. Tucker Elementary School in Alexandria, Virginia, asked the first questions. I promised them I would find and write the answers.

Matt Spangler shared his research for *Out of Obscurity*. James Pratt, 366th Infantry Regiment historian (whose father, Captain Charles A. Pratt, served with Tucker in Italy 1944-1945) and Frank Cloud, who was a 2nd Lieutenant in Cannon Company when Tucker was the commanding officer, helped build the military timeline. Steve Ackerman gave me critical leads that sent me off in unexpected, rewarding directions.

Audrey Davis from the Alexandria Black History Museum and George Combs from the Special Collections Branch at the Alexandria Library checked the manuscript for historical accuracy. They also shared illustrations from their collections. Senator Henry L. Marsh, III, told me stories from his 30-year friendship with Samuel Tucker and checked to make sure what I had written was correct. He also took the time to write the Foreword.

S.W. Tucker's second cousin Sandra Slaughter and Alexandria local historian Lillian Patterson provided photographs. Ferdinand Day, former Chairman of the Alexandria School Board and a Tucker family friend, provided information.

In the beginning, when I had only a plan and chapter outline, Gail Baker, Kathy Lacey Silcox, Pat Brown, and Yvonne Narcisse Green were the first readers and encouraged me to move forward.

Finally, my husband, Steve, through countless revisions, has been my sounding board and patient supporter.

Many thanks to each of you.

ABOUT THE AUTHOR

Nancy Noyes Silcox was the first librarian at Samuel W. Tucker Elementary School in Alexandria, Virginia. She selected and ordered all the school library's books for when the new school opened in 2000. Mrs. Silcox retired from that job in 2011. Then she decided to write a children's biography about Samuel Wilbert Tucker. She hopes the story of Mr. Tucker's life will inspire children to love reading and research as much as he did, and to continue the pursuit of equality for all Americans.

Nancy Noyes Silcox, Taylor Sutton, and Henry L. Marsh, III, posed in front of a photograph of S.W. Tucker displayed during the book's launch at Alexandria Black History Museum on September 14, 2013.

INDEX

COLOPHON

Content composed in Garamond Premier Pro, typeface designed by Robert Slimbach in 2005.
Printed on a 70# Williamsburg Offset using a Xerox digital printer.
Bound in a 12 pt Carolina produced on an Indigo 5600 Digital Press.